Normee Ekoomiak

ARCTIC MEMORIES

Henry Holt and Company • New York

Thanks to Lillian Robinson, Dr. Brian Dobbs, Bela Kalinovits, Phil Surguy, Leo Flaherty, Rolf Roemer, Katolic Utatnaq, the Baffin Divisional Board of Education, the Ontario Arts Council, the Canada Council, and the Multiculturalism Sector of the Department of the Secretary of State of Canada, without whose help this book would never have been published.

Library of Congress Cataloging-in-Publication Data
Ekoomiak, Normee.   Arctic memories / Normee Ekoomiak.   English and Eskimo.
Summary: Text in both Inuktitut and English describes a now vanished way of life for the Inuit.
1. Eskimos—Juvenile literature.   2. Eskimo language—Texts—Juvenile literature.
[1. Eskimos.   2. Eskimo language materials—Bilingual.]   I. Title.
E99.E7E38   1990   998'.004971—dc20   89-39194
                    971.9

ISBN 0-8050-1254-0 (hardcover)
10 9 8 7 6 5 4 3 2
ISBN 0-8050-2347-X (paperback)
10 9 8 7 6 5 4 3 2

First American edition, published in hardcover in 1990 by Henry Holt and Company, Inc.
First Owlet paperback edition, 1992
Printed in the United States of America

ARCTIC MEMORIES

NDAMEE EKOOMIAK.

ᐃᑉᒍ ᐃᓗᐊᓂ

ᓄᑕᕋᐅᔪᖕᒥᒍᓐᓂᖕ ᐃᑉᒍᒥᒐᒥᔭᕝᓴᐅᔭᑦᐳᖕ ᐅᑭᐅᖕᑎᓐᒍ
ᐊᒻᓗ ᐅᑭᐅᖕᔪᖕᓯᖕᓯᐅᒃ ᑐᐱᕐᒪᐸᓕᖕᒧᑕ.
ᐃᑉᓗᓐᑕᐅᖕᑉᑐᒃ ᐃᖕᑐᐊᖕᑐᐅᖕᑐᑉᓯᓐᑉ ᐊᑐᖕᕿᑦ.
ᐅᑭᐅᖕᑕᖕᒍᒥ ᓯᐱᑐᔭᖕᑉᑐᖕ ᐅᑭᐅᑉᑐᑦ. ᐃᖕᖕᓯᖕᓱᓄ
ᐊᒻᓗ ᑕᑉᓄ. ᓯᖕᖕᑉ ᑕᑦᖕᐱᖕᑐᖕᑦ ᑭᖕᑕᓂ
ᐅᐱᖕᖕᒃᔪᑉᖕᖕᐅᒃ, ᖑᐅᖕᒪᖕᒃᔭᑉᖕᓄ ᐅᖕᓄᑉᑉᒃᓄᓂᖕᖕ
ᐅᑭᐅᖕᑉᑭᖕᖕᐅᒃ ᖕᓂᖕᓄᑉᖕᑉᒍᐊᓂᓄᑉ ᑭᑉᖕᐊ ᐱᓐᓄᖕᖕᑐᔪᑉ
ᖕᓐᖕᑉᖕᓄᑕ ᐃᑉᒍ ᐃᓗᐊᓂ. ᐅᖕᖕ ᐊᑕᑕ ᖕᓇᖕᔪᐊᑕᔪᖕ
ᐅᓐᖕᓯᖕᑉ ᖕᓇᖕᔪᐊᖕᐱᖕᒥᖕ ᓄᐅᐱᖕᖕᑐᐅᖕᐊᖕᔭᖕᖕᓂᖕᖕᒃ. ᐅᖕᖕ
ᐊᐊᐊ ᒥᖕᔪᖕᑉᖕ ᐊᖕᓃᐅᖕᑉ ᐊᖕᒃᖕᓄᖕ ᑐᐱᖕᑐᐅᖕᑉᖕᓄᐊᓂ.
ᐅᖕᖕᑭᖕᔭᖕᖕᓄᓂ ᑕᐊᖕᖕᑉᖕᑐᖕᑉ ᑖᐊᖕ ᑐᐱᖕ. ᐃᑉᒍ ᐃᓗᐊᖕᐊ
ᖕᑭᓐᖕᖕᖕ ᓂᐅᑉᖕᖕᑉᑐᖕ ᐱᖕᖕᓄᖕᓄᑉᖕ. ᑖᐊᑕ ᑕᐊᖕᖕᑉᖕᑐᖕᑦ
ᖕᑭᓐᖕᖕᖕ ᐊᒻᓗ ᐅᖕᖕᒍᖕᑉᖕᖕᑉᖕᓄᑕ ᐊᖕᖕᒍᖕᑦᖕᓐ.
ᓯᓐᖕᖕᖕᓐᐊᓂᑕ ᖕᑭᓐᖕᖕ ᖕᒪᖕᑉᐅᑉᖕᖕᓄᓂ ᐃᑉᒍ
ᐅᖕᖕᐊᐊᑉᐊᖕᑕᐅᖕᖕᓄᑕᖕ. ᖕᑭᐱᖕᖕᑉᖕᓄᖕ ᔪᖕᔪᖕ ᐊᖕᒃᖕᓄᑕᑕᖕᓄᑕ ᑕᖕᑕᐊ
ᐅᑕᖕᖕᑐᑕ ᓄᑭᑉᖕᑭ ᐅᖕᑕᖕᖕᑉᖕᖕᓄᖕᑉᑕ ᐊᓂᖕᖕᑭᑕᑭᖕ ᓄᖕᐱᖔᐊ
ᐊᖕᖕᓄᑉᖕᑉᖕᖕᓄᑉ ᐊᖕᑕᓂᖕᖕᓄᑕᖕᖕᓄᖕᒍᖕᑕᑕ.

In the Iglu

"Iglu" means house. When I was small, we
used to live in a snow house in the winter
and in a tent the rest of the year. During the
long winter up North, there is little sun and
it is always dark. We stay inside and do our
work and play. Here the father is carving a
soapstone sculpture for sale at the co-op. The
mother is sewing together seal skins to cover
a tent. When it starts to get warm, the snow
house will melt. We will build a tent to live
in, and we will move with it from place to
place when we hunt for food. Inside the iglu
there is an oil lamp on three legs. It is for
light and for heat. But when we go to sleep,
we put out the lamp, and then it gets cold,
so we must all sleep together to keep warm.
The kids sleep in the middle, between their
parents.

ᐅᑭᐅᖅᑕᖅᑐᒥ ᐅᐱᓐᖑᒥ

ᑐᖅᕐᑎᓕᖃᕙᐅᑦ ᐊᒻᒪᓗ ᑎᒃᑕᐅᕐᖕᐅᓗᓂ ᓯᖅᓯᓐᕐᔪᑦ. ᑎᖕᕙᑦ ᑎᑭᕚᑕᐊᓗᑎᐅᕐᑎ ᐅᑭᐅᖅᑕᖅᑐᑦ
ᐃᕝᕐᓕᐅᑎᐊᕐᑐᕐᑎᐅᕐᑎ. ᑎᖕᕙᑦ ᐅᑭᐅᖅᑕᖅᑐᒥᑎᐅᑕᑐᑦ ᓂᖅᖕᔭᑦ ᐊᒻᒪᓗ ᐃᕝᕐᓕᐊᓗᓂᐅᕐᑎ ᐱᐊᒻᕐᖕᖏᖃᑦ
ᐱᓄᕐᒃᔭᐃᑦ. ᓂᓚᕐᑐᑎ ᑎᕐᖕᕿᑎ ᐊᒻᒪᓗ ᐃᐱᖅᖕᖁᖕᓂᑦ ᓄᓄᒥ.

ᓇᓄᖅ ᕿᑐᑎ ᓂᖅᒥᑎ ᕿᖏᖅᑎ. ᐊᓇᓇᕐᖕ ᓇᕐᕈᖅ ᐅᖅᐅᑎᓯᓄᐅᕐᖕ ᓇᕐᕐᐊᕐᖕ ᓇᓄᕐᑕᓄᐅᕐᖕ
ᐅᐃᒪᐃᕐᕐᐊᓄᓂ. ᓇᓄᖅ ᓂᓄᕐᓚᑐᐃᐊᕐᖕᕐᑐᖅ ᓇᕐᕿᖕᑎ ᕿᕐᐊᓂ ᓂᓄᕐᖕᐊᕐᖕᑕᐃ ᐃᖅᓄᐃᑦ ᐊᕐᖕᕐᓂᕐᑎ
ᐃᒪᕐᑎᐅᑕᓂᑦ ᐸᒪᕐᕈᓂᑦ.

Arctic Spring

The ice is breaking up, getting ready to float across James Bay. It will soon be summer, and the Canada geese are flying north to lay eggs to make more Canada geese. If they are born in the South, they are not as healthy. There is too much pollution, and they do not have the right food. They like the North because it's natural for them.

Nanook, the polar bear, is hungry and is looking for food. The mother seal calls the baby seal, and they swim away and are safe. Now the bear has to eat fish. He would like to eat seal, but if he eats too much of it, he will get wild. It is better for bears to eat fish most of the time. Then they can be our friends.

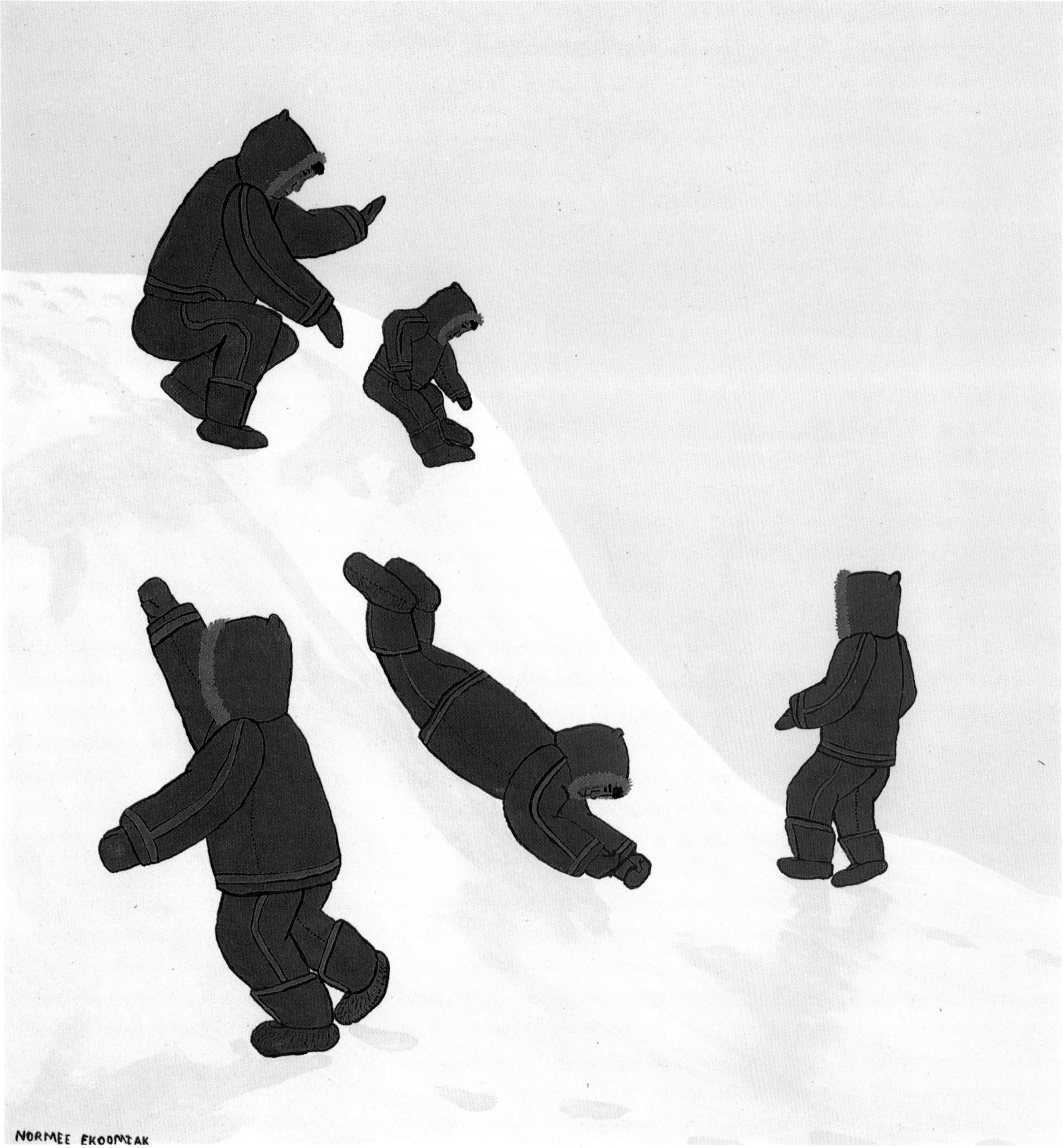
NORMEE EKOOMIAK

ᕿᑎᒃᑐᑦ ᐊᒋᐅᑉᐱᓐᓂᕐᒥ

ᕿᑎᒍᒪᑦᑕᕐᑐᒍᑦ ᓯᓚᒥ. ᑕᕝᕙ ᐊᑕᑕᖓ ᕿᑎᖅᑕᐅᔪᖅ ᐸᓂᖕᒥᓂᒃ ᐊᒻᒪᓗ ᐱᖓᓱᑦ ᐃᕐᓂᖏᑦ ᐊᒋᐊᑉᐱᓐᓂᕐᒥ. ᓯᓚᒥ ᕿᑎᒃᐸᒃᑯᕕᑦ ᑎᒦᑦ ᖃᓄᖕ ᐃᖕᒋᓂᖅᑲᑦᓯᐊᕋᔭᕐᓂᖓᓄᑦ ᐊᒻᒪᓗ ᓱᖕᒋᑦᓯᐊᓗᓂ.

ᐃᒡᓗᖃᖅᑐᓂ ᐊᐳᒥᑦ ᐅᖁᑦᑎᐊᖅᑐᖅ ᐃᓗᐊᓂ. ᐱᖕᓯᐊᓂᒃᑳᖕᒐᑦ ᐊᐳᑕᐃᔭᕐᓗᒍ ᕚᖕᒐ ᑭᓯᐊᓂ ᐊᓂᓇᖕᑐᖕ.

Playing on a Snowbank

We love to go outside and play. Here three boys and a girl are playing with their father on a snowbank. They all slide down, and then race to get back to the top and do it all over again.

Inside an iglu there is not very much space. You cannot stay inside for a long time, not even during a snowstorm. But if you go outside to play, then your body will always be healthy and normal.

Also, someone has to go outside the iglu after a snowstorm to dig the people out.

NORMEE EKOOMIAK.

ᔨᑯᒥ ᐃᖅᑲᑕᐊᕐᓂᖅ

ᐃᓗᐊᓄᒃᑦ ᐱᖅᐸᓂᖅᑳᖕᓘᑦ ᐅᒪᔪᑦ ᑕᒃᑯᐊ ᑐᒃᑐᐃᑦ, ᓇᐲ
ᐊᒻᓗ ᐊᐃᐱᑦ ᓇᓂᕐᓂᖅ ᐊᕐᓲᓇᐳᑦ. ᓂᖅᐱᓕᖅᑲᑎᔪ
ᑭᕐᐊᓂ ᐱᑕᖅᖢᕼᔪᖕᓘᑦ ᐃᖅᓪᒃᕐᒧᕋᖅᑐᑐᑦ.
ᐊᕍᐊᑕᐅᖅᑦᓚᑕᐅᔉᑦ ᐃᖅᔪᓇᕐᔅᖅᖢᓇᖑ ᐃᖅᔪᒃᐱᖅᓂᑦ.

ᐊᕐᓇᓗᖅ ᑖᑳᓪᔪᖅ ᐃᓕᖅᓂᑦ ᑲᓚᕐᖠᔪ
ᐃᖅᔪᓪᕇᐊᖅᕼᕐᐊᖅᖢᔉ. ᑭᕐᐊᓂ ᐃᓗᐊᓄᒃᑦ
ᐃᖅᔪᖅᕐᐃᓇᕈᖅ.

ᐅᒪᔭᖅᐳᓇᕋᖕᓘᑦ ᓂᖅᔪᕼᕼᔅᐟᓴᓄᖅᖢᖢ ᓄᑖᒥ
ᑐᑊᑲᖅᕼᖅᕐᐊᖅᑲᓚᕐᖠᔪᑦ. ᐊᕼᔪᓇᖕᑗᑦ ᔮᒪᔉᖕᓄᖅ
ᖅᐅᔉᓕᖅᕼᔪᑦ ᓇᓯᒪᖕᐉᑦ ᐅᒪᔭᕐᑦ.

Ice Fishing

After a snowstorm it is hard to find caribou
and seal and walrus. All of the birds and
animals are gone. Sometimes months go by
before they come back. So the whole family
has to go out fishing, to catch the arctic char,
through holes in the ice. Sedna is good, and
she makes sure there are plenty of fish. But
sometimes it is hard to catch any fish, and
the birds and animals stay away for a long
time. Then the people must move to a new
camp if they are strong enough. Or else they
will starve.

ᐅᖅᐱᒃ - ᐱᒃᑐᕆᑎ

ᐅᖅᐱᒃ ᐅᖅᖃᑕᐅᓯᒪ ᐃᓄᒃᑐᑦ. ᑕᒫ ᐃᓚᕆᓯᒃ ᐃᑲᔨᖃᑦᓗᓂ ᒥᐊᓂᖅᓴᓇᐅᓯᕐᑲᑐᒃ ᐅᒪᔪᓕᒥᒃ
ᐅᐱᐅᖃᑐᒥ. ᐅᐸᓂ ᑕᑯᓄᑦ ᐅᖅᐱᒃ ᐃᑲᔪᑎᖃ ᓯᕿᓂᖅ, ᑕᕿᓗ ᐊᒻᓗ ᐅᓪᓄᐊᑦ.
ᐊᐅᓯᕆᖃᑐᐸᓂᐅᖅ ᐊᑕᑕᖃᐅᒡᒥᒃ ᐊᖕᒍᓇᕐᐊᓯᓂᐊᑎᓪᓗ ᖃᔨᒃᒥᑦ ᐊᖅᓯᓂ ᐊᒻᓗ ᖅᕐᒥᓂᒃ .
ᐊᓇᓇᖅᐅᕐᒥᒃ ᐊᐅᓯᕆᐅᐊᓇᐅᔪᕐᑲᐅᒃ ᓄᑕᓪᖃᑐᒥᒃ ᐊᒪᖃᒥᓂᑦ ᐅᖅᐱᒃ ᒥᐊᓂᖅᔪᒃ ᐊᓂᑦ
ᐊᒻᓗ ᑎᕐᓚᒥᒃ. ᐅᒪᔪᓕᒥᒃ ᐃᑲᔨᓯᖅᓂᑦ ᐃᑲᔪᑎᖅᑲᑐᐊᑦ ᐊᐅᓯᕆᖃᔪᖃᓄᒃ ᐅᐱᐅᖃᑐᒥᑦ.
ᖁᕕᐊᓱᒃᑎᕐᐊᕐᐸᑦ ᐊᒻᓗ ᑐᖅᓯᕐᑲᐅᓗᑦ ᓂᕐᑎᖅᐊᑐᕐᑲᓂᑦ ᑕᒫ ᐃᑲᔨᖅᔪᑦ ᓂᖅᑲᒥᒃ
ᓇᓂᕐᐊᓇᖅᑕᒪᓯᑐᑎᑐᐊᒻᓗᑎᒃ.

Okpik—The Lucky Charm

"Okpik" means "snowy owl." He is our friend, and his spirit protects all of nature in the North. Here you see the owl spirit, with the sun and the moon and the stars. He is watching over a father who is going hunting with his dog and spear, and he is watching over a mother with a baby in the hood of her *amautiq*. Okpik also is the guardian of the polar bear and of the geese. All of the nature spirits work together and watch over the North. We must keep them happy and only kill the right animals or else the spirits will not let us find food.

ᓂᒋ ⊲ᐅᶜᓚᓄ⊲ᖃᐸᐊᒍᖃ

ᐃᓪᑲᶜᓚᖃ ᐱᒪᐅᖢᢣᘏ. ᓱᢣᖃᓚᐅᖃᓐᶜᒍᖃ ᓂᖁᓇᖕᖃᓐᖃᓂ ᒍᐱᖕᐱᢣᓐᖁᓂ. ᒐᒪᶜᒐ
ᓄᒋ⊲ᖃᒪᐅᐅᢣᐅᒍᶜ ᓄᒪᒋ ᒍᐱᖕᐱᖕᒐ ᖃᖕᢣᖕ⊲ᘎᶜ ⊲ᐸ⊲ᓄᶜ, ᒪᐃᒐᶜᶜ ᐅᖃᑊᒥᖃᒍᒍᶜ. ᓇᐸ⊲ᓄᐃᶜ
ᐃᓄᐊᶜ ᐃᒪᐅᢣᒪᐊᖕᓄᖃ ᒐᒣᓇ ᓄᓇᖃᓕᶜᓚᖃᖃ ᐃᓄᶜᐱᓚᐅᖃᒥᖃᓄᶜ. ᓇᐸ⊲ᓄᐃᶜ ᐃᓇᖕᖕᶜ ᐅᖃᓚᖕᖃ
ᓂᒋᖕᓇᖕᒣᖃ ⊲ᐅᶜᓚᓄ⊲ᖃᒪᶜ ⊲ᒥᓚᓇᖃᓄᶜ ᐅᢣᢣᶜᒥ.

ᐃᓪᑲᶜᓚᖃ ᐅᑭᐅᓄᶜ ⊲ᐃᖃᢣᢣᒐᖃᖕᐱᒪᐅᖢᒪᶜ: ᖃᓇᒐᖃᖕᒍᓇ, ᒐᖃᖃᖃᖕᒍᓇ ⊲ᒥᒍ
ᓄᓇᶜᢣⶍᖃᖕᒍᓇ. ᐃᓄᐊᶜ ᐃᒥᒪᖕᢣᒪᐅᖃᶜ ⊲ᐅᶜᓚᓄ⊲ᖕᖃ ᓇᒍᒍᐃᓇᖃᖃ. ᒐᒪᒪᑊᑲᶜᶜ ᐃᓄᐊᶜ
ᢣᶜᢣᘐᶜ ᖃᖕᒪᖁᶜᒍᶜ ᐅᖃᐅᢣᖕᖕᖃᓄᶜ ᒍᢣᘐᖁ⊲ᐅᶜᒍᶜ.

The Body Needs to Travel

This happened a long time ago. There was no food near the village. The people had to travel to a new place, miles and miles across the ice of Hudson Bay. Half of the people did not want to go. They wanted to stay where they were born and grew up. But the other people said the body needs to travel. They had to find the right spot for themselves, where there would be more animals and birds and fish.

This took place thousands of years ago. There was no Canada and no Arctic Quebec and no Northwest Territories. This was how the Inuit went from one place to all of the other places. This is why all of the people who live around the North Pole can understand each other and why they speak languages that are almost the same.

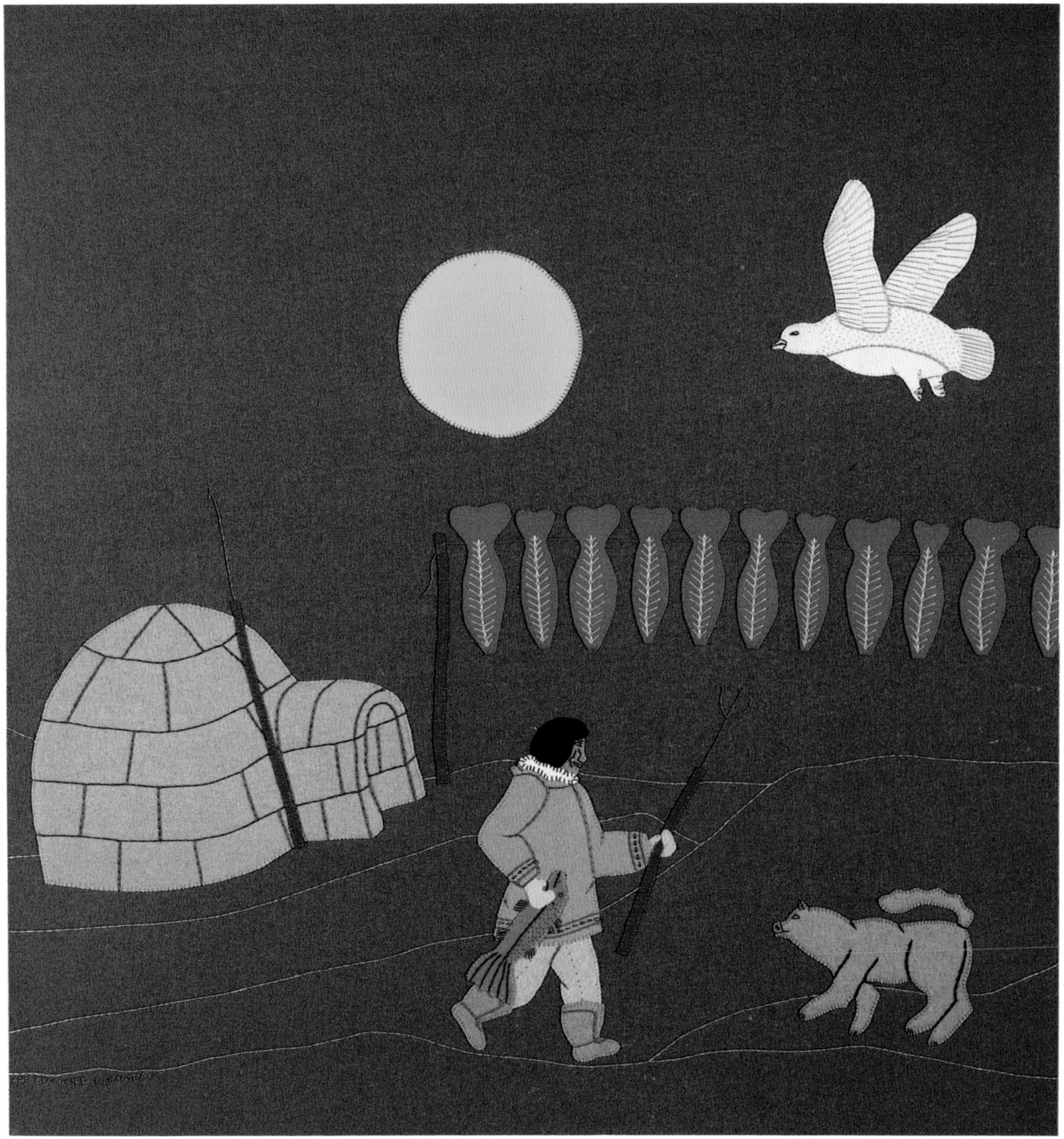

ᐱᖅᓯᓕᐊᑦ

ᐅᐃᓐᖓᒃᑯᑦ ᐊᒻᒪᓗ ᐊᐅᔨᒥᑦ ᐃᓄᐃᑦ ᐃᖃᓗᒃᐸᒃᑐᑦ, ᐱᖅᓯᓕᐊᑎᓴᐅᓪᓗᑎᒃ ᓂᕿᐱᖕᒐᑕᐅᖃᑦᑕᖕᑐᑦ. ᐅᑭᐅᒃᑯᑦ ᖁᐊᑎᓴᐅᓪᓗᑎᒃ ᑐᖁᖕᓯᒪᑦᑎᐊᕐᓗᑎᑦ ᐱᔭᐅᑦᑕᐃᓕᒐᐅᒐᔭᕐᓂᖕᒐᓄᑦ ᓇᓄᕐᓄᑦ, ᐊᒪᕈᓄᑦ ᐊᒻᒪᓗ ᑎᓕᒐᓂᐊᕐᓄᑦ.

ᒥᐊᓂᖅᓯᕗ ᐅᒃᐱᒃ ᑕᑯᔪᖕ ᓇᓄᕐᒥᑦ ᖃᐃᔪᒥᒃ ᐃᓂᖕᑎᓴᖕᑐᖅᑐᖕ ᐃᓄᖕᓄᑦ. ᐃᖃᓗᐃᑦ ᐃᑎᖕᓯᔭᖅᑐᖅᓗᑎᒃ ᐃᓪᓗᒧᑦ ᓇᓄᖕ ᑭᓯᐊᓂ ᓱᑕᐃᖅᐸᑦ.

Hanging Fish

After the fish have been caught, the people have to hang them up to dry and to freeze. They cannot leave the fish under the snow, or the polar bear or wolf or fox could find the fish and eat it.

Here the snowy owl sees the polar bear coming and warns the people. They take the fish with them inside the iglus and wait for the bear to go away. Then they will hang the fish up again.

Okpik watches over his people and makes sure that their food is safe.

NORMEE EKOOMIAK

ᐅᖃᓗᐊᖅ

ᓇᓂᒃᓯᓂᖃᖅᑕ ᓂᕐᔪᑏᑦ ᓂᖅᑐᖅᑎᖅᑎᕐᓂᖓ ᐊᖕᓇᓱᒃᑎᐊᕐᔪᑦ ᖁᓂᖅᑯᑕᐃᑦ ᐊᖕᓇᓱᒃᑎᐊᔾᐅᑎᒥᖅᑐᓂ. ᑕᖕᒪᑐᐃᓐᓇᓂᖅᐊᕐᖕᓂᒥᒃ ᐃᑉᓗᑕᐅᔾᐊᒃᑐᔾ ᓯᓴᖅᖅᐅᖅᑐᔾᐊᕈ ᐊᖕᓴᑎᐅᖅᑐᔾ, ᑭᓯᐊᓂ ᓯᓴᖅᖅᐅᖅᖂᖕᓴᕐ ᐅᖅᖅᐊᓴᐅᔾᐊᒃᓱᓐᖅ ᓴᓇᖅᑐᔾ ᐊᐳᒥᔾ.

ᓇᓂᖅᖂᖅᑕᓐᖅ ᔾᐊᖅᐊᖅᓱᑎᐊᒥᖅ ᐅᑎᖏᓐᖅ ᐃᓕᒥᔾ ᐅᖅᖂᐊᔾᖅᖅᑐᔾ ᒪᔾᖂᔾ ᐊᖅᐊᐃᔾ ᑕᒪᓯᖅᖂᖅ ᐃᓄᐃᑦ ᔾᐊᖅᖕᓐᕆᔾᔾ.

The Shelter

When it is hard to find animals and fish for food, then the two best hunters in the village go out to look for a better place. At the end of the day, they build a shelter for the night. If the weather is bad, they build a whole iglu. But when the weather is not bad, all they need is a windbreak made of two layers of snow blocks. At the end of the next day they build another shelter. This goes on every day until the hunters find a good spot for a new village. Then they go back home, and soon the other Inuit, ten or twenty people, will move to a new place.

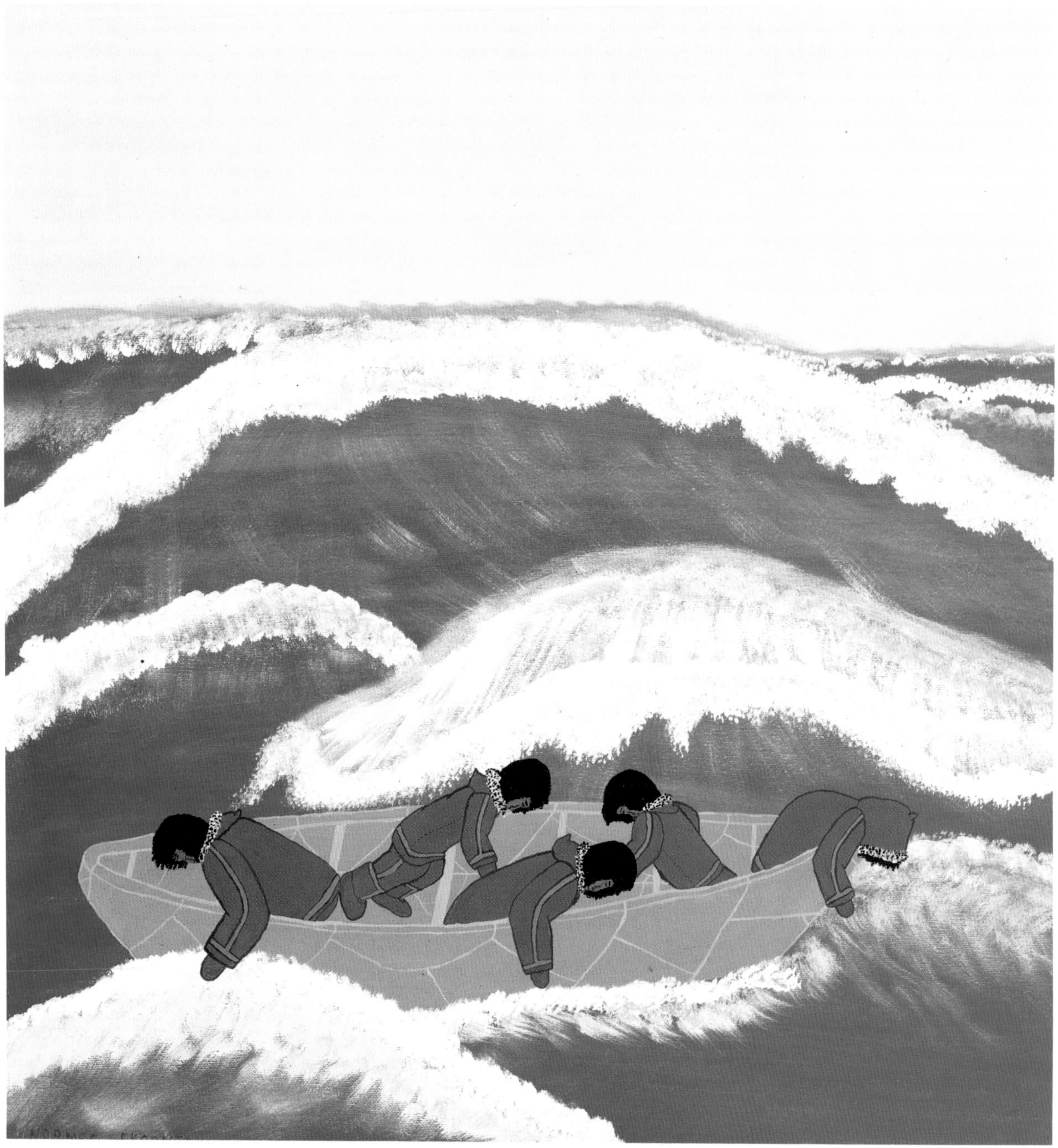

ᐱᕐᓗᒃᑕᐅᓯᒪᔪᐃᑦ

ᑕᐃᑉᓱᒪᓂᒎᖅ ᑕᐃᒃᑯᐊ ᐃᓅᓱᒃᑐᐃᑦ ᕐᑲᐅᔨᔭᐅᒐᒥᒃ ᐱᔭᕆᐊᕐᑲᓚᐅᖅᑎᑕᒥᓂᑦ. ᐃᓚᕋᓱᓚᕋᒥᒃ ᐱᕐᓗᒃᑕᐅᓯᑎᓚᕐᐳᑦ. ᑕᒃᑯᐊ ᐃᓅᓱᒃᑐᐃᑦ ᐃᑭᑉᓗᑎᒃ ᐅᒥᐊᕐᒥᑦ ᐊᒻᒪᓗ ᐅᖕᒐᓱᒃᑐᒧᑦ ᐃᖏᕐᕋᑉᓗᑎᒃ ᓯᕐᑭᓂᖕᒥᐅᒧᑦ. ᓄᓇ ᑕᑯᔭᓐᓇᐃᓕᕐᖢᒍ ᑭᓯᐊᓂ ᐊᑯᓇᕐᑐᐃᓐᓇᕐᓂᑦ ᑕᐅᑐᓐᓇᕐᖢᑎᒃ. ᑕᒃᑯᐊ ᐃᒋᖢᓂᒃᑐᒃ ᐸᐅᑎᖏᑦ, ᓂᕿᖏᑦ ᐊᒻᒪᓗ ᐊᓯᖏᓪᓗ ᐱᕐᑯᑎᖏᑦ ᐃᒪᕐᒧᑦ. ᓇᓂᔭᐅᑉᓗᑎᒃ ᐱᖕᒐᓱᓂᑦ ᐱᓇᓱᐊᕈᓰᑦ ᕐᑲᖏᕐᒪᑦ, ᑐᕐᑯᖕᒐᓗᒃᑳᕐᖢᑎᒃ ᑳᖕᓂᑯᒧᑦ.

The Curse

This is a true story. When an evil person learns your name, he can use your name when he does bad things. This is a terrible curse.

Once, some teenage boys went to school in the South. A bad man discovered their names, and then he committed crimes. The police came to arrest the boys and did not believe they were not guilty. So the boys went to jail for something they had not done. When they got out, they were sent back home. They told their parents what had happened. They had been beaten up and sent to jail. This was a terrible scandal and a shame and a curse.

So the boys had to die. They got into an *umiak* and went out into James Bay so far that they could no longer see the land but only the waves. Then they threw their paddles and their food and oil and their warm clothing over the side of the boat. They were found three weeks later. They had all starved to death.

NORMEE EKOOMIAK

ᖀᓯᕐᖁᓗᓂ ᐊᖀᖅᕆᐊᖅᑕᕐᓂᖅ

ᐃᓄᐃᑦ ᖀᑎᒡᕆᓂᖅ ᐊᖀᖀᐃᕿᑐᖀ ᓂᖀᑕᖀᖀᔨᐊᖀᔪᖀ
ᐊᒡᓗ ᐱᓕᕆᐊᒡ ᐱᖂᓕᖅᑕᐅᖀᖀᑐ. ᖀᓯᕐᖁᕿᓯᓂᖅ
ᐊᖀᖀᐃᐊᖀᖀᖀᓯᓂᖅ ᓇᔭᓲᖀᒡ ᖄᒡᕿᓄᑕᐅᕆᐊᖀᖀᔪᓂ
ᑭᕐᐊᓯ ᑕᑲ ᐃᓄᖀ ᑐᖀᖂᑐᐊᖀᖀᓯᖀ ᐊᖀᕿᒡᖀ, ᑕᐃᒪ ᑕᑲ
ᐃᓄᖀ ᓯᓚᖀᖀᕐᖀᔪᖀ.

ᑕᑲ ᐃᓄᖅᕿᐊᒡᓗ ᖀᑎᖂᖀ ᖀᓯᕐᖀᑕᓂᖂᑦ. ᑕᐃᖀ
ᖀᓯᕐᖀᕿᕐᖀᕐᑑᖀ ᓯᓚᖀᖀᕐᖀᔪᖀ.

High-Kick Game

When there is a lot of food and there is nothing else to do, the Inuit make up games to
play.

In the high-kicking game, the pole is raised
higher and higher until only one person can
kick the ball. That person is the winner. Another boy is playing the hopping game. Here
you hop for as long as you can. This is a
contest, and whoever hops the longest wins.
The other boy is doing a push-up and trying
to pick a stick up with his mouth. His body
must not touch the ground.

These games are fun, but they also make the
body strong.

ᑯᐱᕙᒐᒃ ᐃᕐᑕᕐᔅᑕᐅᓂᕿ

ᑯᐱᕙᒐᒃ ᐃᕐᑕᕐᔅᑕᐅᓂᕿ ᕿᑯᐱᐊᓇᒡᕿ. ᑕᐅᒃ ᑕᵃᓇ ᓂᐱᐊᕐᕪᕈᕿ ᑯᐱᕙᒐᒃ ᐃᕐᑕᕐᔅᑕᐅᕐᕿ.
ᐊᓄᓇᕝᑊᒐᕿ ᓄᕝᒪᓄᕐ. ᑕᵃᓇ ᕿᓄᒡᕪᕿ ᓄᑕᕐᓄᕐ ᐱᒍᕐᓇᓇᕿᕿ ᑭᕿᐊᓄ ᕿᑯᐊᓄᕋᑕᐅᒍᐃᓇᕿᕿ.

Blanket-Toss Game

Blanket tossing is great fun. Here a girl is being tossed up in the air. The wind is
blowing through her long hair. This game makes the children stronger, but it is
just for fun, to have a good time.

ᐊᔅᒐᖅ

ᐃᓄᐃᑦ ᐊᔅᑲᑉᒪᕐᑕᖅᑐᐃᑦ ᓴᓇᑐᐊᖃᓴᓐᑦ ᐊᒻᒪᓗ ᐅᑕᕐᕃᐅᐊᓴᓐᑦ ᐊᖅᓗᕐᒦᑦ. ᑕᑦᓱᓂ ᐊᕝᓯᒥᑦ
ᐊᔅᑲᓇᐊᕐᕃᐊᑦ ᖃᕐᓯᒥᑦ. 22-ᖅᒐᓚᖅᓗᓂ ᐊᔅᑲᓇᐊᓕᖅ ᑭᕐᐊᓂ ᐃᓄᖅᑐᐃᑦ ᐱᐊᓕᓂᖅᑲᐅᕃᐊᑦ
ᐊᑦᓂᐅᓗᐊᖅᑐᒥᑦ ᐱᐊᓂᒍᕐᖃᓕᖅᑐᑦ. 200-ᓂᑦ ᐊᕐᐊᕆᖅᑐᐃᑦ ᖃᓄᐃᑐᐅᐊᓴᓐᑦ ᐊᒻᒪᓗ ᖅᑎᒐᕐᖅ
ᐊᔅᑲᑦᕃᖃᐅᖅᑐᑦ.

The String Game

The Inuit like to make figures of things and animals with string. In this picture the boys are getting ready to make the shape of a kayak. It will take twenty-two separate steps, but the boy's fingers will move quickly and it won't take them long. In all, the people have over two hundred shapes to make and games to play with string.

ᓯᕗᓪᓕᕕᓂᕐᐳᑦ ᐊᖑᓇᓯᒃᑏᑦ

ᐅᕙᓂ ᐊᕐᑎᒥ ᑕᑯᒃᓴᐅᔪᖅ ᐃᒻᒪᑲᓪᓚᒃ ᐅᒥᖕᒪᐅᔭᖅ ᐅᑭᐅᖅᑕᖅᑐᒥᐅᑕᕕᓃᑦ ᐅᑭᐅᑦ ᐃᒻᒪᑲᓪᓚᑦ ᑕᐃᑦᓯᒪᓂ ᐃᓄᐃᑦ ᓇᐃᑦᑐᑯᓗᑎᓪᓗᑎᑦ. ᐊᓯᖕᒋᑦ ᐆᒪᔪᑦ ᑖᒃᑯᐊ ᑐᒃᑐᑦ ᓇᓄᐃᑦ, ᐊᒪᕈᐃᑦ ᐅᕿᓗᓐᓃᑦ ᕐᑭᒻᒦᑦ ᐱᑕᕐᑲᖕᒋᑎᓪᓗᑎᑦ ᓯᓚ. ᐃᓄᐃᑦ ᐱᑕᖕᓯᓪᓗᑎᒃ ᐅᒥᖕᒪᐅᔭᕐᓂᑦ ᓴᓪᓚᖕᑕᐅᓯᒪᔪᒥᒃ ᓂᕐᑭᑕᕆᔭᒃᓴᒥᓂᑦ.

ᒥᖑᐊᖑᐊᕐᑯᒃᑯ ᑕᓐᓇ ᐃᒻᒪᑲᓪᓚᒃ ᐅᒥᖕᒪᐅᔭᕐᒥᑦ ᕐᑲᐅᔨᒪᔪᕐᑲᓚᐅᕐᑯᒪ ᐱᑕᕐᑲᓕᓚᐅᕐᓂᖕᖓ. ᐅᑭᐅᖅ ᐊᑕᐅᓯᕐᒥ ᓇᓂᓯᓚᐅᕐᓯᒪᔪᑦ ᕐᑭᕐᑭᔪᒥᒃ ᐱᐊᕐᑯᓗᖕᒥᑦ ᐅᒥᖕᒪᐅᔭᕐᒥᑦ ᐅᑭᐅᖅᑕᖅᑐᒥ. ᑕᐃᒪ ᒫᓐᓇ ᐱᓯᒪᔭᐅᔪᖅ ᑐᕐᓈᓐᑐᒥ.

Ancestral Hunters

This picture is about the woolly mammoth, thousands of years ago when the Inuit were not very tall. There was no caribou, no polar bear. There wasn't any wolf and there wasn't any dog. So the people have trapped a woolly mammoth in a pit and they are killing it, because there is nothing to eat. When I painted this woolly mammoth, I just knew it was there. Then, one year later, they found a frozen baby woolly mammoth from the Ice Age up in the Northwest Territories, and right now they have it here in Toronto.

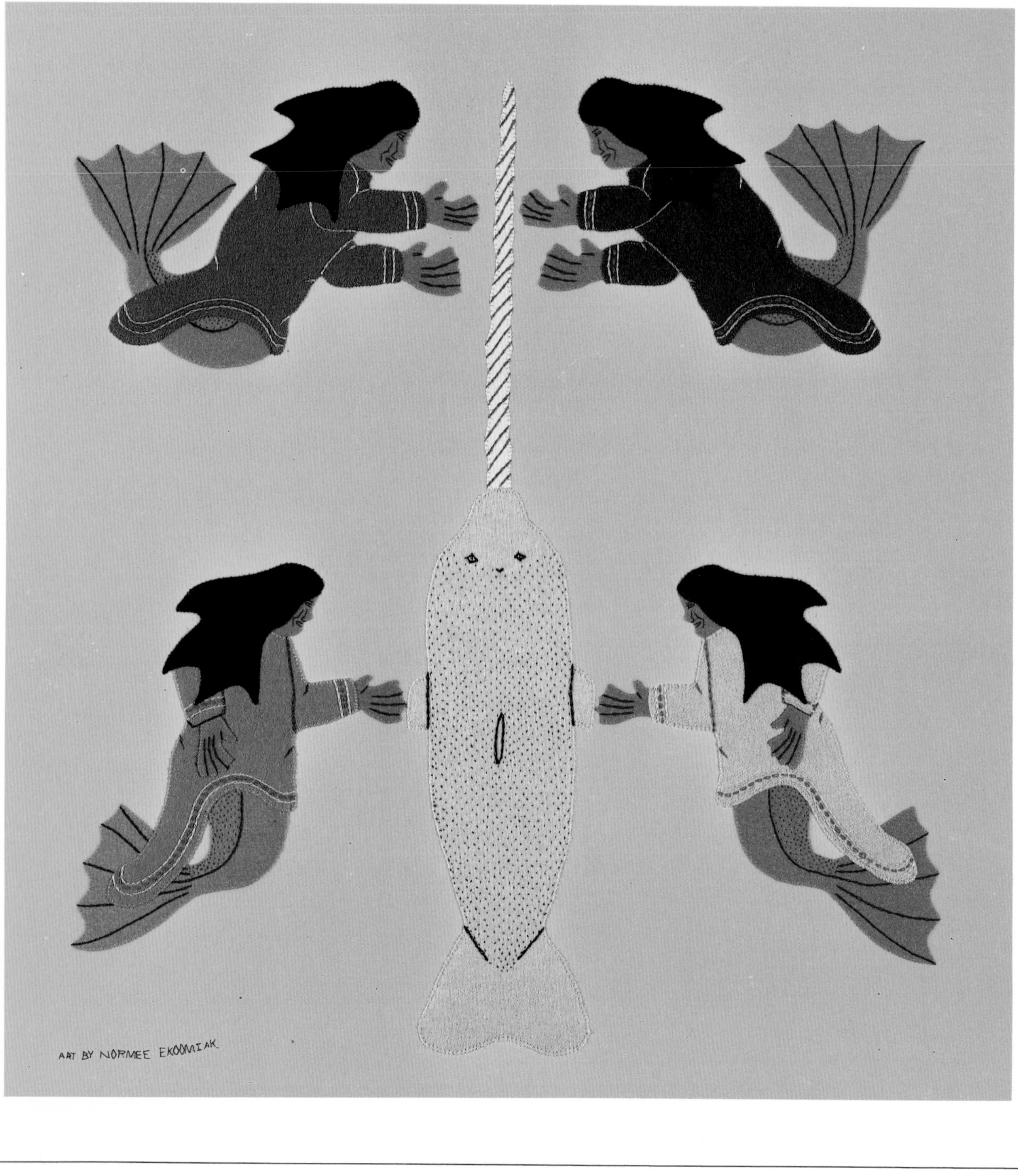
ART BY NORMEE EKOOMIAK

ᐊᕐᓇᕐᔪᐃᓐᓇᐃᑦ ᐊᒻᒪᓗ ᑑᒑᓕᒃ

ᐊᕐᓇᕐᓗᒃ ᑕᑲᓐᓈᓘᒃ, ᐃᒪᕿᒥᑦ ᑲᒪᔾ ᑕᓐᓇ ᐊᕐᓇᕐᓗᒃ ᐊᒻᒪᓗ ᑕᓐᓇ ᓇᔭᖏᑦ ᐃᒪᕿᒥᑦ ᑲᒪᔩᐅᔪᑦ. ᐊᕐᓇᑦᓗᒃ ᑕᑲᓐᓈᓗᒃ ᐱᖑᖏᑦᓯᓚᐅᖕᐳᖕ ᐅᓛᒍᓗᒃᑖᓂᑦ ᐃᒪᕿᑐᓗᒃᑖᓂ.

ᐊᕐᓇᕐᔪᐃᓐᓇᖕ ᐱᕐᓗᒃᓯᔅᖏᖏᓚᑦ ᑕᓇᐅᒥᐅᑕᕐᓂᑦ ᐊᖑᓇᓱᒃᐸᒃᑐᓂᑦ.

Mermaids and the Narwhal

We believe that just off Cape Jones, a long time ago, a father threw his daughter over the side of a boat. She was frightened and held on to the side of the boat. So her father cut off her fingers. She sank to the bottom of the water, where she became the Sedna, the sea goddess who is now a mermaid. All of the animals of the sea—the fish and the polar bear and the seal and the narwhal—were created from her cut-off fingers.

Sometimes it is dangerous in the water. A polar bear can swim out too far and then Sedna must help him back to shore. She cannot use her hands, because her fingers have been chopped off. Sedna uses her mind to make the animal turn back toward shore. The skin of the narwhal is soft and smooth. Sedna touches it and plays with it and rubs it. That is because the narwhal, who is like a king, is her son.

The mermaids will not bother people who go hunting on the sea. But if the people kill the wrong animal—anything that is on land, like wolf, fox, rabbit, ptarmigan—the mermaid will not help them. Because these people did the wrong thing, the mermaids could kill them if they wanted.

ᑯᕐᐃᑐᕆᐅᐸᒃ ᐃᕐᓂᐊᖂᓂᖅ
(ᐊᖅᑭᓯᒪᓂᖅ)

ᐃᓄᐃᑦ ᐅᒃᐱᕐᔪᐊᓗᒍᓐᒃ. ᐃᖅᖁᓂᒃ ᐅᒃᐱᕐᑭᖅᒍᓐᒃ
ᐊᒡᒪᓗ ᓂᖅᔪᐊᕐᒃᖅᒍᓐᒃ ᓄᓇᒥᐅᑕᓄᒃ ᐃᓄᖕᑎᕐᕆᖅᓄᒃ
ᒥᐊᓂᕐᕈᐅᖅᓱᓄᒃ. ᒫᓇ ᐃᓗᖕᑎᒃ ᐃᓄᐃᑦ
ᐃᖅᕐᓴᐊᖅᑐᑕᑕᑐᓕᖅᒍᓐᒃ, ᐳᕐᑭᑎᓇᒃᔪᓕᒍᓐᒃ, ᐅᐸᔪᓇᐉᕐᒃ
ᐸᑕᐊᔪᒃᓇᒃ. ᒫᓇ ᐅᒃᐱᓇᑉᒃᖅᖅᕐᔭᕐᕆ
ᕆᒍᓂᖅᒍᓐᒃ.

Nativity (detail)

The Inuit are a very religious people. We
have our own religion, and we worship the
spirits of nature who protect us. At the same
time, we are Roman Catholic or Anglican or
Protestant or even Baha'i. I believe that what
is in this picture is true.

ᑯᕐᐃᔅᑐᕋᐃᐅᐃ   ᐃᕐᓂᐊᔫᓂᖅᑭ

ᐅᒃᐱᕆᔭᖃᖅᐳᖕ ᑕᐁᓇ ᓄᑕᕋᖅ ᔨᓲ ᐃᓄᑕᐅᓐᓂᖅᑭ ᑕᐁᓇ ᐱᕐᔪᑎᕐᓪᓄᒍ ᐊᑉᓯᕐᖅᓂᖕᓕᒃ ᑲᑎᖅᓱᕐᐃᓕᑦ
ᐃᓄᐃᑦ ᓯᑕᕝᐊᕐᒥ. ᐅᕕᓇ ᓄᑕᕋᖅ ᔨᓲ ᐃᓄᖕᖃᒃᓄᑦ. ᐃᓄᐃᑦ ᐊᐃᑯᒻᑐᖅᒐᐃᑦ ᑐᓄᑉᕐᐊᖃᓐᓄᑦ,
ᐱᐅᖅᕼᕐᐅᑦᐊᑉᓄᖃᓄᑦ, ᒻᓪᑕᐅᑉ ᒻᓪᖃᖃᓄᑦ, ᖁᐱᖃᓄᑦ ᐊᒻᓗ ᑲᖕᖃ ᐊᖕᓇᑕᐊᑉᓂᒻᑦ. ᑕᐁᓇ ᖁᕐᒥᖅ
ᐊᒻᓗ ᓇ̇ᓄᑦ ᐱᐊᖅᖕᓗ ᒫᓐᖃᖅᕐᐱᕐᖅᖕᓕᑦ.

ᑕᐁᓇ ᐃᕐᓂᐊᔫᓂᖕᓕ ᓇᓄᐊᐃᑯᑯᑦᖅ ᐅᕐᓄᓐᐊᖅ ᑲᓚᖃᓐᐅᕐᑦ. ᒪᕐᖂᖅ ᐅᖅᐱᒃ ᐊᒻᓗ ᒪᕐᖂᖅ ᐊᓄᖕᖅ
ᐱᐅᖅ̇ᔫᖕ, ᑎᒍᒪᕐᐊᖂᒻᑦ ᓇ̇ᑉᕐᖅᑎᒻᑦ ᒫᓐᖃᖅᖑᕐᐃᑦ ᓄᑦᕐᒻᑦ ᔪᕐᔪᒻᑦ. ᑕᐁᓇᓗ ᐊᒻᓗᖅᖕ ᑭᖕᖕᒥᒻ ᒍᖅᖃᖅᒻᑐᒻᑦ
ᓂᖕᑉ̇ᓪᒻᐅᖅ ᑕᖅᒻᓗᑦ. ᒍᖕᖅᑕᐅᑉᐊᑉᓪᓪᒻᖕᓐᖕᑊ ᐊᒻᒪᒻᓄᑦ ᐃᓄᖕᒻᓄᑦ ᐊᒻᓗ ᐅᕝᔭᖅᖄᒻᓄᑦ
ᑕᐃᑯᖕᑉᐅᕐᒻᐅᑉᓪᓪᒻᖕᓐᖕᑊ ᓄᑦᕐᔪᑦ ᔪᕐᔪᑦ.

Nativity

I believe that a Baby Jesus is born everywhere, to every different group of people in the world. Here Jesus is a baby Inuk. The people are bringing him their gifts, good luck charms: a narwhal tusk, a blanket, and a spear for hunting. The dog and the polar bear cub are there to watch over him and protect him.

Up in the sky the North Star and a great shooting star are signs of the miracle. Two snowy owls and two angels, with candles from the church, are there to watch and protect. The wolf on the hill is howling the good news to the moon, and it will be heard by more people, more children, and more wild animals, who will all come to Baby Jesus.

ᓚᐳᕐᑎᐅᕝ   ᐱᓂᖅᑲ

ᑕᐁᓇ ᒥᖅᓱᒐᐅᕐᕦ ᓂᔅᖃᕝᒐᓕᐊᖅ ᑐᓂᕈᑎᐅᕝᓕᓇᒧ ᐃᓄᕐᖄᖕᑖᓂᒄ ᐅᐱᐅᖅᑲᖓᒥᖅᑖᓂᒄ ᑕᕐᒐᕝᕕᑲ
ᓚᐳᕐᑎᒄᕝ 100-ᓂᒄ ᖄᔅᖃᐳᓂᓕᑖᓂᖅ.   ᐊᕐᕐᖅᑐᑕᐃ ᖃᓴᖕᓂᑦ ᑎᖕᒐᐃ ᑐᖅᖅᖕᑐᑦ ᐊᕐᕐᖅᑐᑕᐃ
ᕿᕐᕝᑐᑖᖃᖃᐃ ᐃᖄᐃᒄ ᐅᐱᐅᖅᑐᒥ ᐊᒥᐊᒄᖄᖕᐳᓂᖕᑦᒄ ᖃᒪᕿᑦᐊᔅᖕᓂᒄ ᓚᐳᓂᒐᒄ ᐊᒋᓚᓌ
ᖅᑯᖕᐊᕐᕐᐊᖕᔅᓌᓂᒄᒄ.   ᑕᐁᓕᓌ ᐅᕝᐱᒄ ᐅᐃᐃᐱᕐᐊᖕᐊᖕ ᓚᐳᓂᒐᒄ, ᐅᕝᐱᐅᕝ ᐱᓂᖅᑲ, ᑕᐅᑐᕝᖕᖅ
ᖄᓴᑐᐊᖄᕐᓂᒄᒄ ᐊᒄᖄ ᖕᖄᕝᖕᖅᓂᒄᒄ.

The Spirit of Liberty

I made this wall hanging as a gift from the native people of North America when
the Statue of Liberty was one hundred years old. The different-colored geese flying
by stand for all of the races of man. They have all come to North America to enjoy
liberty and happiness. Watching over them and the Statue of Liberty is Okpik, the
spirit owl, who sees everywhere and who sees everything.

Editor's Notes:

The Inuit

There are approximately a hundred thousand Inuit, or Eskimos, in the world today. Some live in Greenland (Denmark), some in Siberia (the Soviet Union), and some in Alaska (the United States). In Canada there are twenty- to twenty-five thousand Inuit. Most of them live in the part of the country known as the High Arctic. It is a region of snow, ice, and rock, swept by dry winds and dangerous blizzards. There are no roads or big cities. Yet the Inuit have managed to survive and prosper in this environment.

Traditional Inuit were hunters and trappers. They built houses of snow and ice in the winter, and tents of animal hide in summer. They went where game was most plentiful.

Many people think that Eskimos still live in iglus and travel only by dogsled. Some do, but most have incorporated modern housing and vehicles like snowmobiles into their lifestyle as well. On a hunting trip, for instance, both a snowmobile and a dogsled might be used—the dogsled because it will not run out of gas, and the snowmobile because it can go faster. Modern Inuit life is often a mixture of the old and the new.

Among the Inuit there are many different groups, called bands, tribes, or nations. Each of these groups lives in a different territory; each has its own language dialect and its own culture. Some of these groups are the Mackenzie, or Inuvialuit; Copper; Netsilik; Caribou; Iglulik; and Ungava.

The Language

"Inuk" is the Eskimo word for "person." There are two plural forms: "inuuk" ("two persons") and "inuit" ("three or more persons"). "Inuit" is this group's own word for itself. It is usually translated as "the people."

In the Inuit language, Inuktitut, sentences are formed by making additions to a root word. For instance, the sentence "He was not allowed to hunt caribou" can be said in Inuktitut by a single word: *Tuttusiurqujaulaungituq.*

The Inuit did not have a writing system until the nineteenth century. Missionaries traveling in the Arctic created one because they wanted to translate the Bible into Inuktitut. They devised a system based on the one used by the Cree Indians. It is still in use today. The text of *Arctic Memories* is written in both English and Inuktitut.

Inuit Art

During this century many changes have taken place in the Arctic. Inuit life once centered on hunting, trapping, and fishing. But now there are not enough whales, caribou, or bear to support this traditional way of life. The Inuit have had to find different ways to make a living.

Many Canadian Inuit now earn their livings as artists. They often operate small co-op businesses where they work together to create and market their art. Traditionally the Inuit are skilled carvers and needleworkers. Many of today's artists make carvings or work with fabric. Since the 1950s they have also become excellent printmakers. Many fine prints are created in Inuit co-ops.

Through artists like Normee Ekoomiak, the Inuit traditions continue and are enhanced. Mr. Ekoomiak draws and paints. He also creates embroidered and appliqued wall hangings. Through his subjects—and his techniques—Mr. Ekoomiak ensures that the Arctic of his memory will live for generations to come.

The author in his own words:

WHO I AM

I am an Inuk. I was born in a place of magic: at Cape Jones. This is where James Bay empties into Hudson Bay, on the east shore, the Quebec side.

My people are the Inuit of James Bay in Arctic Quebec. My father's people came from the country around Povungnituk. My mother's family came from Great Whale River. Right across the water are our cousins on the Belcher Islands. We call ourselves "Inuit," which means "people." Our neighbors, the Cree Indians, call us "Eskimos." This means "people who eat raw fish."

I know all of the spirits of the land animals and the birds and the fish and the sea animals. I know their names and I can understand them and I can speak to them. I have heard the owl and I have heard the bear and I have heard the Sedna singing. When I was small, I had a sickness in my ears and it did not go away properly. So now it is hard for me to hear what other people are saying, but I can still hear the spirits.

I can remember everything. I grew up at Fort George in my grandfather's tent, which had a wooden frame and was covered in canvas and with seal skins. It was about ten feet by twenty feet. My grandfather taught me about Inuit ways and about how to do my art. My father and mother and six brothers and seven sisters lived with us. I went to school at the mission there.

In 1971 I had to leave Fort George. I was too lonely. So first I went to Ottawa to stay with my sister and her family. I did my art and learned to eat some of the food of the South. Then in 1972 I came to George Brown College in Toronto and later went to the New School of Art. After that I made many paintings and drawings and wall hangings, which I sold to friends and to art galleries. I wanted to go back to Fort George, but the Hydro-Quebec James Bay Project has flooded the area and a new settlement called Chisasibi is now in the place where Fort George used to be. My North is not there anymore. It is only in my memory.

I live and work in the South now. I am an Inuk of the city.